PRAYER AND
STUDY GUIDE

THE
POWER
OF A
Praying
Wife

STORMIE OMARTIAN

HARVEST HOUSE™ PUBLISHERS

EUGENE, OREGON

Cover by Koechel Peterson & Associates, Minneapolis, Minnesota

THE POWER OF A PRAYING® WIFE PRAYER AND STUDY GUIDE
Copyright © 2000 by Stormie Omartian
Published by Harvest House Publishers
Eugene, Oregon 97402

Library of Congress Cataloging-in-Publication Data
ISBN 0-7369-0317-8

Printed in the United States of America

03 04 05 / BC / 15 14 13

THIS BOOK BELONGS TO

_____

Please do not read beyond this page without permission of
the person named above.

Contents

How Do I Begin?

Welcome to this great adventure of becoming a praying wife. Don't worry if you have mixed emotions during this process. We all do. It may not be easy, but it will be rewarding. That's because *prayer works!*

What You'll Need

This prayer and study guide is divided into a 30-week plan for use in personal or group study. You will need to have the book THE POWER OF A PRAYING WIFE. You will also need a Bible. Make sure the Bible you have is one you are not hesitant to write in.

About Your Answers

The questions in this study are sometimes very personal, and your answers should be completely honest. Therefore, keep this book in a private place. If the answers you need to write down are lengthy and have the potential to be hurtful to other people, write them in a separate blank notebook that you can keep private or destroy later. Your answers are not for anyone else to read or for you to be tested on. They are to help you see the truth and be able to think clearly about each area of prayer focus. They will assist you in determining exactly what you and your husband's prayer needs are, and they will show you how to pray. Try to write something for each question or direction, even if it's only one sentence.

How to Proceed

In group study, it's good to follow the order in this book so the group will have the same focus when it comes together each week. In individual study, don't feel you must continue in the same order if there are pressing issues you need to pray about right away. In every instance, however, "The Power" and chapter 1: "His Wife" must be the first chapters read before proceeding.

In a Group

In group study, after you have read the appropriate chapter in THE POWER OF A PRAYING WIFE book and answered the questions in this PRAYER AND STUDY GUIDE on your own, the leader will bring the group together and go over each question to see what insights God has given you and the other women as they feel led to share them. Although you may or may not want to share personal information in the group, please share what God is showing you and speaking to your heart when you find this happening. It's good for you to say it, and it's helpful for other people to hear.

For Clarity

When referring to God, the pronouns *Him* or *He* will be capitalized. When referring to your husband, the pronouns *him* and *he* will not be capitalized.

How to Pray a Scripture

Frequently, you will be asked to write out a specific Scripture as a prayer over your husband. To help you understand how to do that, I have included an example of how I pray Ephesians 1:17,18 over my husband. Look it up in your Bible, and then see what I have done below:

> Lord, I pray that You, the God of our Lord
> Jesus Christ, the Father of glory, will give to

Michael the spirit of wisdom and revelation in the knowledge of You, so that the eyes of *Michael's* understanding will be enlightened; so that *Michael* will know what is the hope of his calling, that *Michael* will know what are the riches of the glory of Your inheritance in the saints.

What If My Husband Doesn't Know the Lord?

The Bible says a husband and wife are one, and an unbelieving husband is sanctified by the believing wife. Because of this, the wife of an unbelieving husband can pray all the same prayers and speak the same Scriptures over him as a wife could over a believing husband, and expect to see answers to prayer. The most important and ongoing prayer, of course, is that your husband's eyes be opened to the truth of God and he be led to receive Jesus as his Savior.

Your Role

Your role is to become an intercessor for your husband. *An intercessor is one who prays for someone else and makes possible the ability of that person to respond to God.* What a great privilege to be used by God in that way!

WEEK ONE

Read "The Power" and chapter 1: "His Wife"
from THE POWER OF A PRAYING WIFE.

Remember as you answer the following questions that God already knows the truth. He is not going to be shocked or disappointed in your answers, so don't you be either. Don't condemn yourself for the areas where you need improvement. We all have them. Simply take each question before the Lord and ask Him to show you the truth and help you become the woman and wife He wants you to be. Believe me, I know how hard this chapter is, but when you get through it, the rest will be easy. What happens to your heart here will pave the way for success in seeing answers to your prayers.

1.   Read Matthew 19:3-6 in your Bible.
      Underline verses 5,6. Do you believe that you and your
      husband are one in the sight of God? Are there places in
      your marriage where you and your husband are not
      working together as a team? List those areas. Write a
      prayer asking God to make you and your husband more
      unified in these areas. Ask Him to show you what you
      can do to facilitate that unity.

2.   Read Luke 10:19 in your Bible and underline it.
      You don't have authority over your husband, but whom
      do you have authority over?

3.   God has given you the authority to take a stand against
      any negative influence in your marriage. Is there any
      area in your marriage where you see that the enemy has
      gained or is trying to gain a stronghold? List below.

4. Are there any places in your marriage where you feel hopeless? List these below. Bring them before the Lord and confess your hopelessness. Remember, confession is not to make you feel condemned; it's to help you acknowledge your error before God so He can free you from it, and so the devil can't paralyze you with it. Write a prayer asking God to give you the faith you need to believe that He is your hope and will answer your prayers.

5. Read Joel 2:25 and underline it in your Bible.
    What things do you see depleting life out of your marriage? What does God promise He will do when things have been eaten away from our lives?

6.   Do you believe in God's ability to heal wounds? To renew love in your heart? To restore your marriage relationship to all it should be? Why or why not?

7.   Read Matthew 10:39 and underline it in your Bible. Do you trust God enough to answer His call to lay down your life in prayer for your husband? Why or why not? If not, write a prayer asking God to help you trust Him enough to make this commitment.

8.   Read Matthew 12:25 and underline it in your Bible. Is there any issue over which you and your husband are seriously divided? How do you feel about it?

9. Do you have any anger, unforgiveness, hurt, or disappointment toward your husband? Explain why. Even if you have good reason for feeling the way you do, confess those negative thoughts as sin and ask God to set you free from them. I know this is hard if you feel justified in your feelings, but this prayer of confession and repentance must come first before you can begin praying for your husband with a right heart and see answers to your prayers.

10. Do you ever feel like you don't want to pray for your husband? Explain why. Write a prayer asking God to help you desire to pray for God's best to be poured out on your husband. (This may be a prayer you have to pray every day for a while, so don't worry if you haven't sensed an immediate answer.)

11. Is there anything for which you need to ask your husband to forgive you? Ask God to show you if there is anything for which you need to repent (an attitude, action, are of neglect, and so on). As He reveals it, write it down. Write a prayer asking God to give you the courage, strength and humility, to ask your husband for forgiveness and to communicate your love and a desire to change.

12. Tell your husband you are going to start praying for him every day in a new and positive way, and ask him to share with you any prayer requests he has. Write down what his reaction was and what requests he shared.

13. Do you see your husband as anything less than a beloved son of God? Explain. Write out a prayer asking God to help you see your husband through His eyes.

14. Look up Proverbs 21:19 and underline it in your Bible. Are there any issues in your marriage where you find yourself registering the same complaint or criticism over and over? List those. Write a prayer asking God to show you when to speak about each matter and when to just keep silent and pray.

15. Is there any sensitive matter that you know you need to speak to your husband about, but you fear what his response might be? What is that? Write a prayer asking God to show you what you are to say and when to say it. Ask God to prepare your husband's heart to hear it.

16. Read Psalm 62:5 and underline it in your Bible.
    Are there any expectations you have of your husband that he is not living up to? What are they? Write a prayer asking God to show you where your expectations of your husband don't coincide with the reality of who he is. Tell God you will put your expectations on *Him* so *He* can meet your needs.

17. Read Ephesians 5:33 and underline it in your Bible. Is there any area in which you have lost respect for your husband? Explain. Write a prayer asking God to reveal ways you may have demonstrated a lack of respect for your husband. As He reveals them, confess them as sin and ask God to help you see your husband the way *He* sees him.

18. Read Galatians 5:22,23 and underline it in your Bible. Do you have any habitually negative ways of responding to your husband that need to be changed? What are these? Write them down. Ask God to give you revelation about this. Then write down next to them which fruit of the Spirit you need in order to eliminate the negative mindset and habits of response.

19. Read Proverbs 31:10-31 in your Bible. Ask yourself the following questions without expecting perfection:

    Are you a trustworthy wife?

    Yes _____ Need Improvement _____

    Are you an asset to your husband?

    Yes _____ Need Improvement _____

    Do you work diligently to make a home in which he can be comfortable and happy?

    Yes _____ Need Improvement _____

    Are you careful and wise with money?

    Yes _____ Need Improvement _____

    Do you take care of your physical health and appearance?

    Yes _____ Need Improvement _____

    Are you a giving person?

    Yes _____ Need Improvement _____

    Are you prepared for the future?

    Yes _____ Need Improvement _____

    Do you make sure your family members have their needs met?

    Yes _____ Need Improvement _____

    Do you generally move in wisdom?

    Yes _____ Need Improvement _____

    Are you always loving and kind?

    Yes _____ Need Improvement _____

    Is your relationship with the Lord alive, intimate, growing, and strong?

    Yes _____ Need Improvement _____

Without being hard on yourself, write a prayer asking God to help you with each area in which you need to improve and enable you to become the wife He wants you to be.

20. Pray the prayer out loud on pages 44–46 in THE POWER OF A PRAYING WIFE. Include all the specific needs, desires, and hopes from your own heart.

Whew! You got through chapter 1. If you are at all like me, you will probably have to keep referring back to this chapter whenever you find your attitude less than what it should be. For months I had to keep confessing my bad attitude every time I prayed for my husband, so don't feel badly if you have to do that, too. In fact, according to the mail I have received since THE POWER OF A PRAYING WIFE first came out, we are not alone in this. So don't give up, and you *will* see good results.

WEEK TWO

Read chapter 2: "His Work"
from THE POWER OF A PRAYING WIFE.

1. Is your husband successful in his work? Does he need to
    find work? Does he need to find work that is more suit-
    able for him? Explain. Write a prayer asking God to open
    up doors of opportunity for him to be successful in the
    work God created him to do.

2.   Does your husband have a tendency toward laziness?
      Workaholism? Somewhere in between? How could his
      work habits improve? Explain. Write a prayer asking God
      to remove any obstacles from your husband's mind or
      emotions that cause him to be unbalanced in his work
      habits.

3.   Is your husband a good provider? How could you better
      support his efforts to provide for his family? Explain.
      Write a prayer asking God to bless the work of your hus-
      band's hands so that his work will increase and he will be
      rewarded accordingly.

4. Read Ecclesiastes 3:13 in your Bible and underline it. Is your husband's work fulfilling to him? Does he enjoy the good of his labor? Why or why not? Write a prayer asking God to help your husband find fulfillment in his work, whether it means moving him into something different than what he is doing now, or giving him a new sense of purpose about the work he already has.

5. Is your husband living up to his potential? Are there gifts and talents in him that are not being used or are not being used to the glory of God? Does he know what his gifts and talents are? Explain. Write a prayer asking God to open up doors for your husband which utilize the gifts God has placed in him.

6. Read Proverbs 22:29 in your Bible and underline it.
    Has your husband been unable to excel in his work? Has
    he been properly recognized and appreciated for his
    work? Explain. Write a prayer asking God to enable your
    husband to excel in his work and be recognized for it.

7. Does your husband do his work with a sense of purpose
    and fulfillment, or with feelings of frustration, aimless-
    ness, or unfulfillment? Explain. How do you think you
    could pray about this for him?

8. Does your husband get along well with his coworkers? Are the people over him happy with what he does? Is he shown respect by the people he works for and with whom he has daily interaction? Describe his work relationships in general. How could you support him in prayer?

9. Is there a difficult person your husband has to work with, or an unpleasant work relationship that could be depleting your husband's strength and patience? Explain. Write a prayer asking God to transform this relationship or to change your husband's perspective and enhance his patience.

10. Pray the prayer out loud on page 53 in THE POWER OF A PRAYING WIFE. Include specifics about your husband's work.

WEEK THREE

Read chapter 3: "His Finances"
from THE POWER OF A PRAYING WIFE.

1. Is your husband a financially responsible person, or is he sometimes irresponsible with money? How do you feel about that? Explain.

2. Read Luke 12:29-31 in your Bible and underline it. Does your husband suffer from anxiety about finances? Describe. In light of this verse, what should he be doing about it? How could you pray about this?

3.   Read Malachi 3:10 in your Bible and underline it.
      Does your husband have a heart to give as God directs in
      this Scripture, or does he need to move into this area of
      obedience to God? Explain. Write a prayer asking God to
      speak to him about this matter.

4.   Is your husband miserly, overgenerous, or somewhere in
      between? Explain. How would you like to see that
      changed? Write a prayer asking God to give your hus-
      band a generous spirit controlled by the will of God.

5. Read Psalm 41:1-3 in your Bible and underline it.
    In light of this Scripture, the blessings that come from
    giving to the poor cannot be ignored. Are there any
    blessings you feel you are lacking because you or your
    husband are not giving to the poor? Explain. Remember
    that if your husband doesn't disapprove of *your* giving,
    this speaks well for *his* generosity, too.

6. Read Matthew 6:21 in your Bible and underline it.
    Is your husband's focus on his finances or on serving the
    Lord? If you don't know, ask God to show you, and write
    down what He reveals.

7. Do you feel your husband makes financially sound decisions? Explain. Write a prayer asking God to give you and your husband wisdom as to how to handle your finances. Pray that neither of you will spend money irresponsibly or make poor financial choices, but that you will have God's revelation about *all* financial decisions.

8. Have you and your husband been financially depleted for an oppressively long time? Does it seem that every time you start to get ahead, something comes along to steal finances away? Explain and be specific. Write a prayer asking God to end financial loss, strain, poverty, or lack of blessing in your lives. Tell Satan he cannot steal and rob from you and your husband any longer.

9. Is there anything you could do to help relieve the financial burden on your husband? Ask God to show you, and write down what He reveals. If you are working to support the family also, write a prayer asking God to bless the work of your hands and make it fruitful.

10. Pray the prayer out loud on pages 57–58 in THE POWER OF A PRAYING WIFE. Include specifics about your finances.

WEEK FOUR

Read chapter 4: "His Sexuality"
from THE POWER OF A PRAYING WIFE.

1. Do you feel your sexual relationship with your husband is good, not good, or somewhere in between? Why? Regardless of what it is now, write a prayer asking God's covering over it and blessing on it.

2. How would you like to see your sexual relationship with your husband change? Explain. Write a prayer asking God to make it what you want it to be.

3. List the top ten priorities in your life. These are the things that occupy your time, attention, and energy, such as children, work, friends, church activities, and so on. In this list, where does your relationship with your husband fall? What does this list reveal to you about your priorities?

4. If your husband *is* at the top of your priority list under God (where he should be), is the sexual aspect of that relationship a priority? If it hasn't been, what are the reasons for that (illness, marital strife, financial worry, emotional stress, lack of interest, busy schedule, children, exhaustion, and so on)? Write a prayer asking God to help you make any changes necessary in order to make your sexual relationship with your husband the priority it should be.

5. Do you look forward to intimate times with your husband? Has your husband done anything that has turned you off to his physical advances? Explain. What do you believe would improve your physical relationship?

6. Read 1 Corinthians 7:4,5 in your Bible and underline it. Are you sexually available for your husband at his request? Is he available for you? Does the frequency of sex between the two of you usually depend solely upon him? Upon you? Is the frequency with which you come together mutually agreed upon? Have you ever kept yourself from being available to him, when you could have done otherwise? Write a prayer asking God to help both of you be in complete unity about this aspect of your relationship. Confess any times you kept yourself from your husband when you could have done otherwise.

7. Do you ever sense frustration in your husband over your sexual relationship? What do you understand his frustration to be? What could you do to help alleviate that frustration? Write a prayer asking God to give you revelation about that and help you to do what is necessary to make your sexual relationship with your husband better.

8. Has your husband ever been tempted toward infidelity? Have you? Has that temptation ever been acted upon? If yes, how has this affected the way you relate to each other? If no, how do you keep yourselves from temptation? Write a prayer asking God to protect both of you from immorality.

9. Do you keep yourself sexually attractive to your husband? Do you try to stay healthy, fit, clean, fragrant, attractively attired, and rested? Is there anything you could do to improve yourself physically, emotionally, mentally, or spiritually? Write a prayer asking God to bless you with an inner and outer attractiveness to your husband that keeps him from being attracted to anyone else.

10. Pray the prayer out loud on pages 65–66 in THE POWER OF A PRAYING WIFE. Include specifics related to your intimate relationship with your husband.

WEEK FIVE

Read chapter 5: "His Affection"
from THE POWER OF A PRAYING WIFE.

1. Read 1 Corinthians 7:3 in your Bible and underline it.
   Do you feel your husband is affectionate enough toward
   you? Explain.

2. Does your husband feel you are affectionate enough toward
   him? Are you sure? What could you do to improve that?

3. What does your husband feel is the best way for you to communicate love toward him? (Ask him if you are not certain.) Are you able to do that?

4. Do you have children? Do you feel you and your husband have modeled for them a marriage that is filled with an abundance or a lack of affection? How do you think it will affect them in their own marriages? If you have modeled a lack of affection, would you both be willing to change?

5. Write a prayer asking God to help you and your husband demonstrate healthy affection toward one another so that your children will learn to do the same.

6. Have you or your husband taken one another for granted in any way that has eroded your tendency to be affectionate toward one another? Has one of you assumed incorrectly that the other one doesn't need affection? Explain.

7. Have other distractions caused you or your husband to not take the time necessary to show affection toward one another? What could you do to change that?

8. Read 1 Corinthians 10:24 in your Bible and underline it. In what ways could you seek your husband's well-being over your own?

9. Is there some act of affection you could show toward your husband today that would pleasantly surprise and bless him? What is that? (If you can't think of anything, ask God to help you.) Are you willing to do that? Write down the results after you've done it.

10. Pray the prayer out loud on page 72 in THE POWER OF A PRAYING WIFE. Include specifics related to you and your husband's relationship.

WEEK SIX

Read chapter 6: "His Temptations"
from THE POWER OF A PRAYING WIFE.

1. Read Luke 22:40 in your Bible and underline it.
    What does Jesus specifically direct us to do in this Scripture?

2. Is there anything in your husband's life that is a tempta-
    tion to him? What is that? Write a prayer asking God to
    free your husband from anything that tempts him away
    from God's perfect will for his life, and to keep him from
    any temptation in the future.

3. Is there anything in *your* life that is a temptation? What
    is that? Write a prayer asking God to keep you from en-
    tering into anything that tempts you away from God's
    perfect will for your life.

4. Read James 1:12 in your Bible and underline it.
    If you sense that another person is becoming a tempta-
    tion to your husband, pray for this individual to be taken
    out of your husband's life. Whether something like this
    has happened to him or not, write this Scripture as a
    prayer over your husband, substituting his name for "the
    man" and for all pronouns.

5. Read James 1:13-15 in your Bible and underline it. How are we tempted? What do our own desires produce? What is the ultimate result?

6. Read Mark 14:38 in your Bible and underline it. Even if your husband is not habitually tempted by anything in particular, temptation is always a possibility for anyone, especially where our flesh is weakest. Does your husband have a weakness in the flesh that you feel *could* become a snare from the enemy? If so, what is it? If you are not aware of anything, ask God to reveal it to you. Write a prayer asking God to protect him in this area.

7. Does your husband have any godly men in his life to whom he can be accountable on a regular basis? List those men below and pray that they will be a blessing to your husband. If he doesn't have that kind of man in his life, write a prayer asking God to bring godly men to him and enable him to develop relationships of accountability with them.

8. Read Galatians 5:16,17 in your Bible and underline it. What does the flesh lust against? How can you keep from fulfilling the lust of the flesh? Write a prayer asking God to help you and your husband walk in the Spirit and not in the flesh.

9. If your husband were to fall into temptation even after you have been praying, what do you think your reaction might be? What do you pray your reaction *would* be?

10. Pray the prayer out loud on pages 77–78 in THE POWER OF A PRAYING WIFE. Include specifics related to your husband's temptations.

WEEK SEVEN

Read chapter 7: "His Mind"
from THE POWER OF A PRAYING WIFE.

1. Does your husband frequently experience fear, depression, or anxiety? Explain.

2. Does your husband ever believe lies about himself? Explain.

3.   Do you believe that God has given you all authority over the enemy on behalf of your husband? How then would you address the enemy regarding the lies he speaks to your husband's mind?

4.   What are the two most powerful weapons against the attack of lies upon your husband's mind (page 82)?

5.   Read Hebrews 4:12 in your Bible and underline it.
     In light of this verse, how could speaking the Word of God over your husband in prayer help to reveal wrong thinking?

6. Read 2 Timothy 1:7 in your Bible and underline it. Write out how you might speak this verse, inserting your husband's name and claiming it as his right.

7. When we praise God for the promises He gives us in His Word, it paves the way for them to come to pass. Write out a praise to God for your husband's sound mind.

8. Read 1 Corinthians 2:16 in your Bible and underline it. Write out this verse as a prayer over your husband to help him bring every thought under God's control.

9. Read Mark 12:30 in your Bible and underline it. Write out this Scripture as a prayer, inserting your husband's name.

10. Pray the prayer out loud on page 84 in THE POWER OF A PRAYING WIFE. Include specifics about your husband's struggles of the mind.

WEEK EIGHT

Read chapter 8: "His Fears"
from THE POWER OF A PRAYING WIFE.

1. List below any fears you know your husband has. Do you share any of the same fears? Explain why.

2. Ask your husband if there are any fears he has which he would like you to pray about for him. Are there any that he mentioned which you did not put on your list above or that you were not aware of until now?

3.   How have your husband's fears affected you?

4.   Read 1 John 4:18 in your Bible and underline it. What takes away fear?

5.   Who is the only one in the universe who has perfect love? Whose love should you pray will penetrate your husband's life?

6. What is the only kind of fear we are supposed to have (page 89)?

7. When you have the fear of the Lord, what does God promise to do (page 89)?

8. Read Psalm 27:1 in your Bible and underline it.
   When God is your strength, of whom should you be afraid?

9.   Read Psalm 34:4 in your Bible and underline it.
      In light of this Scripture, how could you pray for your
      husband so that he would be set free from fear?

10.   Pray the prayer out loud on pages 89–90 in THE POWER
      OF A PRAYING WIFE. Include specifics regarding your
      husband's fears.

WEEK NINE

Read chapter 9: "His Purpose"
from THE POWER OF A PRAYING WIFE.

1. Do you have a sense of what your husband's purpose in
    life is, or who God created him to be? What is that? If you
    don't know, write a prayer below asking God to show you.

2. Does your husband have an understanding of God's call
    on his life? What is his understanding of it? Explain.

3. Do you feel your husband is fulfilling the call God has on his life? Is he living in the purpose for which God created him? Explain.

4. How would you like to see your husband better move into what God has called him to be?

5. Read Ephesians 1:17-19 in your Bible and underline it. Write that Scripture as a prayer over your husband, inserting his name.

6. Read Psalm 20:4 in your Bible and underline it.
    Write out that Scripture as a prayer over your husband.

7. Have you sought God about the call on your life? If so, what is it? If not, write a prayer to God asking Him to reveal it to you.

8.   The call on your life and the call on your husband's life will never be in conflict. If they seem to be, ask God to clarify that to you. It may have to do with timing. How do you see God working out His call on both of your lives? If you don't know, write out a prayer asking Him to reveal it to you.

9.   If your husband is already moving in the call God has on his life, the enemy will try to cast doubt and discouragement into his soul. Do you ever see that happening? How can you support him in prayer to help keep that from happening?

10.   Pray the prayer out loud on pages 95–96 in THE POWER OF A PRAYING WIFE. Include specifics about your husband's purpose and call.

WEEK TEN

Read chapter 10: "His Choices"
from THE POWER OF A PRAYING WIFE.

1. Do you feel your husband generally makes good deci-
    sions? Why or why not?

2. Do you often see or sense things instinctively that your
    husband doesn't? How does he react to this? Does he see
    or sense things that you don't? How do you react to this?

3. Does your husband ask your advice before making major decisions or choices with significant ramifications? Why or why not?

4. When you give your husband advice, does he weigh it carefully before making any major decision or choice? How does that make you feel? How can your prayers help him to make wise choices?

5. Read Proverbs 1:7 in your Bible and underline it.
   Does your husband seek God before making decisions?
   Does he wait for God's leading before acting? Explain.

6. Read Proverbs 1:5 in your Bible and underline it.
   Write this Scripture as a prayer over your husband,
   inserting his name.

7. Is there any area in which you feel your husband consis-
   tently makes poor choices? Explain. Write a prayer
   asking God to help him make better choices in that area.

8. Read Proverbs 11:14 in your Bible and underline it.
    Are there godly people with whom your husband could
    seek counsel regarding certain decisions he has to make?
    Who are they? If not, write a prayer asking God to send
    godly counselors to your husband.

9. Write a prayer asking God to help these godly counselors
    to impart understanding and direction to your husband.
    Pray also that he will receive it.

10. Pray the prayer out loud on page 101 in THE POWER OF
    A PRAYING WIFE. Add specifics related to your hus-
    band's choices.

WEEK ELEVEN

Read chapter 11: "His Health"
from THE POWER OF A PRAYING WIFE.

1. How would you describe your husband's general health?

2. Are there specific areas of your husband's health that concern you?

3. Are there any specific areas of your husband's physical health that you are concerned about possibly being a problem in the future? Explain.

4. Does your husband have good or bad habits when it comes to taking care of his health? Describe and be specific.

5. Does your husband have good intentions but poor follow-through, good intentions and good follow-through, or does he have no intentions at all when it comes to taking care of his health? Describe.

6. Does your husband have particular habits that bother you because they undermine his health? Explain what they are. Would you describe your attitude about his health habits as being pleasantly patient, cheerfully convicting, or notoriously nagging? Explain.

7. Are there things you have tried to get your husband to do for his health, but he just won't do them? What are they? How does that make you feel when he won't take your suggestions to heart? What do you think he should be doing for his health?

8. Read Proverbs 16:24 in your Bible and underline it. In light of this Scripture, how can you contribute to your husband's health?

9. Read 2 Kings 20:5 in your Bible and underline it. What does this Scripture promise to those who pray fervently?

10. Pray the prayer out loud on pages 105–06 in THE POWER OF A PRAYING WIFE. Include specifics about your husband's health habits.

WEEK TWELVE

Read chapter 12: "His Protection"
from THE POWER OF A PRAYING WIFE.

1. Have you heard of or experienced incidents where you or
    a person you know was saved from disaster because
    someone had prayed? Give an example.

2. Do you believe God will answer your prayers for protec-
    tion on your husband? Why do you believe that?

3.   Read Psalm 61:3 in your Bible and underline it.
     Write this Scripture as a prayer for your husband, in-
     serting his name.

4.   Read Psalm 91:11,12 in your Bible and underline it.
     Write this Scripture out as a prayer for your husband, in-
     serting his name.

5. Do you see any possible dangers in your husband's life that need to be covered in prayer (travel in cars or airplanes, dangers at work, and so on)? List them below. Be specific.

6. Does your husband ever do anything that you consider unnecessarily dangerous? Do you feel he needs to be more careful or stop taking risks? Do you sense dangers he is not concerned about? How do you feel God is leading you to pray about that?

7. Read Psalm 91:1,2 in your Bible and underline it.
   Write out this Scripture as a prayer over your husband, inserting his name.

8. Read Psalm 18:3 in your Bible and underline it.
   In light of this Scripture, how are you and your husband
   protected from any enemy?

9. Do you believe that when you call upon the Lord He will
   hear your prayers and save you and your husband from
   your enemies? Why or why not?

10. Read the prayer out loud on page 109 in THE POWER OF
    A PRAYING WIFE. Include specifics about the protection
    of your husband.

WEEK THIRTEEN

Read chapter 13: "His Trials"
from THE POWER OF A PRAYING WIFE.

1.   Read James 1:2,3 in your Bible and underline it.
     Does your husband find joy in the midst of trials? How
     does he react to tough times?

2.   Do you believe your prayers can make a difference in how
     your husband responds to trials? How so?

3. Read Romans 8:28 in your Bible and underline it.
    Do you really believe that? Why or why not? Is your faith
    strong enough to help your husband find the good in
    tough times? Are you willing to pray him through any
    trial? Why or why not?

4. God uses trials to work His purposes in our lives. How
    can you pray for your husband to not be destroyed in the
    trials he faces without minimizing what God desires to
    accomplish in him through them (page 114)?

5. Is there a certain kind of trial that keeps reoccurring in your husband's life? What is that (problem with work, finances, relationships, and so on)?

6. Read Psalm 55:16,17 in your Bible and underline it. How often do you need to pray when you are in the heat of a battle or trial?

7. Read Matthew 24:13 in your Bible and underline it. Write a prayer for your husband based on that Scripture.

8. Is your husband in the midst of a trial right now? What is it? How can you support him in prayer?

9. Read 1 Peter 1:6,7 in your Bible and underline it. Write this Scripture as a prayer, inserting your husband's name.

10. Pray the prayer out loud on pages 114–15 in THE POWER OF A PRAYING WIFE. Include specifics about any trial your husband is facing.

Read chapter 14: "His Integrity"
from THE POWER OF A PRAYING WIFE.

1. Integrity means to adhere to moral and ethical principles. Do you feel your husband is a man of integrity? Why or why not?

2. Is the man your husband appears to be to other people the same or different than the man you know him to be in private? How so?

3. Is your husband, for the most part, a man of his word? Could he improve in that area? If so, in what way?

4. Read John 16:13 in your Bible and underline it.
    In light of this Scripture, how can you pray for moral and ethical guidance for your husband?

5. Read Proverbs 20:7 in your Bible and underline it.
    In light of this Scripture, what is another important reason to pray for your husband's integrity?

6. Is your husband easily deceived? Have you ever seen him being deceived in any way? Are you concerned that he might be deceived sometime in the future? Explain. Write a prayer below, asking God to open your husband's eyes to the truth so that the enemy will not be able to blind him.

7. Do you believe your husband would ever compromise what he knows to be the right thing to do? Explain. Write a prayer about that.

8. Do you sense there are influences around your husband trying to sway him away from the paths of righteousness? Identify those influences and write a prayer for the removal of them from his life.

9. Any man can be bombarded by the enemy seeking to destroy him. Write a proclamation in Jesus' name that the enemy of your husband's soul will have no power to sway him from moral principles he knows are right.

10. Pray the prayer out loud on pages 118–19 in THE POWER OF A PRAYING WIFE. Include specifics about your husband's integrity.

WEEK FIFTEEN

Read chapter 15: "His Reputation"
from THE POWER OF A PRAYING WIFE.

1. Read Proverbs 22:1 in your Bible and underline it.
   Why do you think God puts such a high value on having
   a good reputation?

2. What are three ways our reputations can be ruined (page
   121)?

3. Have any of the three ways mentioned previously happened to you and/or your husband? Explain.

4. Do you feel your and/or your husband's reputations have been damaged? How so? How do you feel about that? Do you believe God can restore your good name?

5. If you feel that your or your husband's reputations have been damaged in any way, write a prayer asking God to redeem and restore your good names. Whether anything like that has happened to you or not, write a prayer asking God to keep this kind of situation from happening to you in the future.

6.   Read Proverbs 31:23 in your Bible and underline it.
      Do you think a virtuous wife automatically deserves a
      husband who is respected, or does she have an important
      part to play in that happening? What part could she play?

7.   Read Psalm 17:8,9 in your Bible and underline it.
      In these days of lawsuits, it is worth your time and effort
      to pray that such things never bring destruction upon you
      or your husband. How could you pray the above Scrip-
      ture over you and your husband?

8. Gossip can destroy reputations quickly. Write a prayer asking God to protect you and your husband from it.

9. If damaging gossip has already been spread about you or your husband, write a prayer asking God to silence those voices and be your Defender. Ask Him to bring restoration and help you and your husband to forgive the people who gossiped.

10. Pray the prayer out loud on pages 122–24 in THE POWER OF A PRAYING WIFE. Include specifics about your husband's reputation.

WEEK SIXTEEN

Read chapter 16: "His Priorities"
from THE POWER OF A PRAYING WIFE.

1. Read Matthew 4:10 in your Bible and underline it.
    What should be the top priority in your husband's life? In
    your life?

2. Do you feel your husband's priorities are in the right
    order? Explain.

3. Do you feel that you are first, after God, on your hus-
    band's priority list? How does that make you feel?

4. Do you ever feel that you are unprotected, unloved, or uncovered because you are not a priority with your husband? Why or why not? Write a prayer asking God to heal any hurts in this area.

5. Can you think of ways you could set aside time for you and your husband to be alone, doing something he would enjoy? Write down those ideas.

6. Do you ever wish your husband would take time for you alone more than he does? Explain.

7. Do you ever feel your husband puts his children before you? In what way?

8. Does your husband ever feel you put your children before him? Are you sure? If so, what could you do about this? Ask God to help you change that.

9. Read Philippians 2:4 in your Bible and underline it. Does your husband look out for the interests of his family before himself? Do you feel he puts the interests of other people before those of his own family? Explain. How does that affect your family? Write a prayer about it.

10. Pray the prayer out loud on page 129 in THE POWER OF A PRAYING WIFE. Include specifics about your husband's priorities.

Read chapter 17: "His Relationships"
from THE POWER OF A PRAYING WIFE.

1. What are your husband's friends like? Are they godly? Do you feel they are an asset to him or a detriment? Explain.

2. Read Proverbs 12:26 in your Bible and underline it. Are there any people you would consider to be especially bad influences in your husband's life? Does he have any relationships that continually trouble him? Explain.

3. Read 2 Corinthians 6:14 in your Bible and underline it. Does your husband have any close friends or close business relationships with people who are not believers? List their names below and pray for their salvation.

4. Where does your husband find most of his friends (church, work, athletic clubs, and so on)? Do you think it is a good place to meet the kinds of friends he needs?

5. Does your husband have close, mature, believing male friends or mentors who counsel him and encourage his spiritual growth? Does he want them?

6. Does your husband have a good relationship with each of his family members? Is there anyone in particular who is especially troubling for him? Are some family relationships weak or strained? Write a prayer about those relationships.

7. Is your husband part of a men's prayer group or Bible study? If yes, write a prayer concerning his involvement in that group. If no, write a prayer for that to become a reality in his life, no matter how remote that possibility may seem now.

8. Is there any relationship your husband has that is strained or broken because of his unforgiveness? Explain. Write a prayer asking God to convict your husband's heart about his need to forgive.

9. How is your friendship with your husband? Do you think it could be improved upon or deepened? How could you pray to that end?

10. Pray the prayer out loud on pages 134–35 in THE POWER OF A PRAYING WIFE. Include specifics about your husband's relationships.

WEEK EIGHTEEN

Read chapter 18: "His Fatherhood"
from THE POWER OF A PRAYING WIFE.

1. Does your husband ever worry about being a good father? Have you asked him if he does? If he has never been a father, does he want to be? Explain.

2. Did your husband have a good father? What does he say his relationship with his father was like? What is it like today?

3. Does your husband desire to emulate his father as a dad, or does he want to do a better job with his children than his father did with him? Why?

4. Does your husband have a good relationship with each of his children? Why or why not? If he does not have children of his own, does he get along well with other people's children? Does he need prayer about that?

5. Do you feel your husband has bonded with each child? Do you feel you have bonded with each of your children? If you do not have children, explain how you feel about this situation and how you would like to see your prayers answered regarding it.

6. Does your husband ever feel guilty or like he has failed as a parent when he sees something wrong with his children? Explain. If he does not have children, does he feel a lack because of it? How could you pray about that?

7.   What is the best way for a man to become a good father?
      What is the best way to have a father's heart (page 139)?

8.   Read 2 Corinthians 6:18 in your Bible and underline it.
      Does your husband really know God as his heavenly Fa-
      ther? Do you? Explain. Write a prayer asking God to re-
      veal Himself to you both as your heavenly Father.

9. Do you ever feel your husband is more concerned with being a good father than he is with being a good husband? Explain. How does that make you feel?

10. Pray the prayer out loud on pages 140–41 in THE POWER OF A PRAYING WIFE. Include specifics about your husband's ability to be a good father.

WEEK NINETEEN

Read chapter 19: "His Past"
from THE POWER OF A PRAYING WIFE.

1. Is there anything from your husband's past that repeatedly torments him? Describe.

2. Is your husband's past something from which he learns, a part of his life he tries to ignore, or a place where he lives? Explain.

3. Read Philippians 3:13,14 in your Bible and underline it. Do you feel your husband is able to reach forward to all God has for him? How do you think your prayers might help him to do that?

4. Are you concerned that there is anything from your husband's past that could be passed down to your children (alcoholism, divorce, anger, fear, lust, and so on)? Explain.

5. Was there anything that happened in your husband's childhood that is affecting his life today? Was his childhood happy, sad, troubled, carefree, normal, uneventful, full of turmoil, or unstable? Explain.

6. Was your husband ever labeled with unflattering names that have imprinted themselves on his memory and emotions and perhaps colored his image of himself? Explain. Write a prayer breaking the power of those hurtful memories and asking God to heal the wounds.

7. Read 2 Corinthians 5:17 in your Bible and underline it. Does your husband truly understand that he is a new creature in the Lord? Do you? Explain why you do or do not believe this truth. Write out this Scripture as a prayer, inserting your husband's name in it. Then write it out with your name in it.

8. Read Isaiah 43:18,19 in your Bible and underline it. Write below what you are to do about the past. What does God promise if you do that? Do you believe this for your husband? For yourself?

9. Read Ephesians 4:22-24 in your Bible and underline it. Write this Scripture as a prayer, inserting your husband's name. Then put your name in it. Declare it as truth.

10. Pray the prayer out loud on pages 145–46 in THE POWER OF A PRAYING WIFE. Include specifics about your husband's past (and your past, too).

WEEK TWENTY

Read chapter 20: "His Attitude"
from THE POWER OF A PRAYING WIFE.

1. Does your husband frequently have a bad attitude, or is he usually even-tempered and cheerful? Explain.

2. Do events of the day affect your husband's attitude, or is he able to rise above them and cast his cares on the Lord with ease? Explain.

3. Do you react to negativity in your husband? How so? Do you immediately go to the Lord in prayer about it? How could you respond more positively?

4. Has your husband's attitude affected you as a person? How so? Have negative attitudes been brought out in you as a result of his reactions? Explain.

5. Has your husband's attitude affected your marriage in a negative way or a positive way? Explain. How could you pray about that?

6. Read 1 Corinthians 13:2 in your Bible and underline it. Does your husband have a full knowledge of the love of God? Do you feel he has truly experienced God's love in his life? Have you? Explain. How could you pray about that?

7. Read Psalm 100:4,5 and underline it in your Bible. Does your husband know how to do what is described here? Write this as a prayer, inserting your husband's name. Then do it again, inserting your name.

8. Read Proverbs 15:13 in your Bible and underline it. In light of this Scripture, how could you pray for your husband's attitude?

9. Read Matthew 12:35 in your Bible and underline it. Do you see good things or bad things come out of your husband's attitude? How can you use this Scripture to pray over your husband?

10. Pray the prayer out loud on pages 150–51 in THE POWER OF A PRAYING WIFE. Include specifics about your husband's attitude.

WEEK TWENTY-ONE

Read chapter 21: "His Marriage"
from THE POWER OF A PRAYING WIFE.

1. Have you or your husband ever been divorced? If so, write a prayer breaking the spirit of divorce over your lives. If not, write a prayer that a spirit of divorce will never enter into your marriage.

2. Is there divorce in your husband's family, especially with his parents or grandparents? Explain. Write a prayer breaking any generational tie that would cause a spirit of divorce to become part of his life.

3. Is there divorce in *your* family, especially with your parents or grandparents? Explain. Write a prayer breaking any generational tie that would cause a spirit of divorce to become part of your life.

4. Read 1 Corinthians 7:10,11 in your Bible and underline it. Have you or your husband ever viewed divorce as an option which you would consider? Explain. Write a prayer breaking the power of those thoughts of divorce.

5. Has your husband ever committed adultery during your marriage or any previous marriage? If so, write a prayer asking God to deliver him from all the bondage of that sin. If not, pray for the protection, strength, and grace to keep him from ever falling into anything like that—even in thought.

6. Have you committed adultery during your marriage or any previous marriage? If yes, write a prayer of repentance before the Lord and ask for His forgiveness and deliverance from the bondage of that sin. If no, write a prayer asking for the strength, grace, and protection to keep you from ever falling into anything like that—even in thought.

7. Read 1 Corinthians 10:12 in your Bible and underline it. In light of this Scripture, what should you never assume? How does this Scripture inspire you to keep praying for the strength of your marriage?

8. Is there any person or thing that threatens the stability of your marriage? Write a sentence below, taking authority over that threat in Jesus' name and commanding it to be removed from your life. If there is nothing threatening your marriage, write a prayer asking God for protection over your marriage so no person or situation will ever be allowed to harm it.

9. Make a statement below, declaring to your enemy that you refuse to allow anything to come in and destroy your marriage. Declare to God that you will partner with Him and do whatever it takes as far as you are concerned to see that your marriage becomes what it is supposed to be.

10. Pray the prayer out loud on pages 155–56 in THE POWER OF A PRAYING WIFE. Include the specifics of your marriage.

WEEK TWENTY-TWO

Read chapter 22: "His Emotions"
from THE POWER OF A PRAYING WIFE.

1. Is there a negative emotion that you commonly observe in your husband? If so, what is it (anger, depression, fear, and so on)? How does it manifest itself?

2. Read Proverbs 22:24,25 in your Bible and underline it. What happens when we are frequently around someone with a constant negative emotion? (In this example, it's anger.)

3. Do you see from the previous Scripture how important it is for your own well-being, as well as your husband's, to pray for his emotions? Describe how his emotions affect yours.

4. It's good to pray that your husband stop being controlled by his emotions and instead be controlled by what (page 159)?

5. Read Proverbs 21:14 in your Bible and underline it. What is the best gift a wife can give her husband in secret (page 159)?

6. Do you have any negative emotions that are frequently reoccurring? If so, what are they? Why do you think you have them? How could you pray about them?

7. How do your negative emotions affect your husband? What could you do to not be controlled by your emotions?

8. Read Psalm 34:1-4 in your Bible and underline it.
    From this Scripture, what is it we should be doing to combat anger, depression, and fear? How often are we to praise Him?

9. Read Psalm 23:3 and underline it in your Bible.
    In light of this Scripture, do you believe that negative emotions are part of a person's character that can or cannot be changed? Why?

10. Pray the prayer out loud on page 161 in THE POWER OF A PRAYING WIFE. Include specifics about your husband's emotions (yours, too).

Week Twenty-Three

Read chapter 23: "His Walk"
from THE POWER OF A PRAYING WIFE.

1. How would you describe the kind of walk your husband has through life? Does he walk close with God or independently from God?

2. Does your husband have a sense of direction and purpose, or does he wander aimlessly, or somewhere in between? Explain.

3. Read Psalm 84:11 in your Bible and underline it.
   What are the rewards for those who walk in righteousness before God?

4. Read Psalm 1:1; 128:1; Proverbs 10:9; 13:20 in your Bible and underline them. According to these Scriptures, how are we supposed to walk?

5. We are supposed to walk in the_____ and not in the_____ (page 165). Which do you believe your husband walks in most of the time? Why?

6. Do you trust your husband to walk righteously, or do you
   fear he can easily be led off the right path? Explain why
   you feel the way you do.

7. Read Romans 8:5-9 in your Bible and underline it.
   How can we live according to the Spirit? What happens
   when we live in the flesh? How can you be sure that you
   are not walking in the flesh?

8. Read Romans 8:13,14 in your Bible and underline it. What is the ultimate end of living in the flesh? In the Spirit?

9. Read Jeremiah 10:23 in your Bible and underline it. From this Scripture, describe how we are to walk through our lives. How then should you pray for your husband's walk?

10. Pray the prayer out loud on pages 165–66 in THE POWER OF A PRAYING WIFE. Include specifics as related to your husband's walk with God.

WEEK TWENTY-FOUR

Read chapter 24: "His Talk"
from THE POWER OF A PRAYING WIFE.

1. Read Ecclesiastes 10:12 in your Bible and underline it. Do you feel the words that come from your husband's mouth are generally good or sometimes foolish? Have his words ever hurt you? Have you had to forgive him for his words? Explain.

2. Read Ephesians 4:29 in your Bible and underline it. Write this Scripture as a prayer over your husband.

3.   Do you feel your husband is a man of truth? To what degree is he or isn't he? Explain.

4.   Read Psalm 34:12,13 in your Bible and underline it.
In light of this Scripture, what is a good reason to pray for
your husband to be a man who speaks truth?

5. Is your husband a complainer? Does he always see the glass half empty or half full? Explain. Write a prayer asking God to give him a sense of hope, peace, and joy.

6. Does your husband speak too quickly before he thinks or weighs the consequences of his words? How do his words reveal what's in his heart? Explain. How could you pray about that?

7.   Read Matthew 12:37 and 15:11 in your Bible and under-
     line them. Have you ever seen your husband's words
     bring negative results into his own life? Explain.

8.   Read Proverbs 15:23 in your Bible and underline it.
     What can we derive from the words we speak? Does your
     husband need more of that in his life? Do you?

9. Read Proverbs 13:3 in your Bible and underline it. What is the ultimate consequence of not watching what you say? How could you pray this Scripture over your husband? How could you pray it over yourself?

10. Pray the prayer out loud on page 171 in THE POWER OF A PRAYING WIFE. Include specifics about your husband's talk.

WEEK TWENTY-FIVE

Read chapter 25: "His Repentance"
from THE POWER OF A PRAYING WIFE.

1. Read Proverbs 28:13 in your Bible and underline it.
    Does your husband have difficulty confessing his faults?
    What will happen if he doesn't confess his sins? What
    will happen when he does confess his sins?

2. When your husband confesses his faults, do you feel he is
    truly repentant and intent on changing his behavior?
    Explain why or why not.

3. What are the three steps to changing our behavior (page 174)?

   First there is _____, which is _____.

   Second there is _____, which is _____.

   Third there is _____, which is _____.

4. What does true repentance mean (page 174)?

5. Do you feel your husband moves fully in those steps of confession, repentance, and asking forgiveness? With which step does he have the most difficulty? The least difficulty? How could you pray about that? Answer these same questions about yourself.

6. Read Romans 2:4 in your Bible and underline it. What leads us to repentance? What will lead your husband to repentance? What will lead *you* to repentance? How could you pray about that?

7. Does pride ever keep your husband from admitting he is wrong? Do you feel this may have kept him from some of the blessings God has for him? Explain. Write a prayer breaking any stronghold of pride in your husband. Then do the same for yourself.

8.   Are there instances where you believe your husband's true repentance would bring needed healing to you or to someone else you know? How could you pray about that?

9.   Read 1 John 3:21,22 in your Bible and underline it. How will admitting your sins ultimately affect you or your husband?

10.   Pray the prayer out loud on page 175 in THE POWER OF A PRAYING WIFE. Include specifics as related to your husband's repentance.

WEEK TWENTY-SIX

Read chapter 26: "His Deliverance"
from THE POWER OF A PRAYING WIFE.

1.   Is there anything in your husband's life from which you
     know he needs to be set free (alcohol, drugs, pornog-
     raphy, lust, eating disorder, and so on)? Explain.

2.   Read Psalm 50:15 in your Bible and underline it.
     What do you have to do to see God's deliverance happen
     in your life? Do you believe that Jesus is your Deliverer?
     Does your husband?

3. Read Proverbs 24:11 in your Bible and underline it. Does your husband ever do things that seem self-destructive, careless, or dangerous? Explain.

4. Does your husband ever feel hopeless, as if there is no way out of a situation? In what kinds of situations does he feel that? Explain.

5. The ultimate result of feeling that there is no way out is suicide. Has your husband ever had suicidal thoughts? If so, how often and how serious were they? Whether he has had those thoughts or not, write a prayer asking God to keep him free from any suicidal thoughts in the future.

6. Read Psalm 91:14 in your Bible and underline it.
   Often simply by setting our sights on the Lord, having a heart for Him, and living His way, deliverance will happen. How could you pray this Scripture over your husband, trusting that deliverance will happen for him?

7.   Everything from which we need deliverance comes from the enemy. State here again what you have been given over the power of the enemy (Luke 10:19). How do you intend to use that in order to see your husband set free from things that control him? How do you intend to use it for your own deliverance?

8.   Don't hesitate to get mad at the enemy and tell him you will not allow his plans to succeed in your husband's life. Write that below and be sure to state in whose name you have been given authority to make that statement. Do the same for yourself.

9. Read Galatians 5:1 in your Bible and underline it. Because you are one with your husband, you can stand strong with him to resist the power of the enemy whenever the enemy seeks to put him into bondage. How can you address the enemy using this Scripture?

10. Pray the prayer out loud on pages 179–80 in THE POWER OF A PRAYING WIFE. Name the specific things for which your husband needs deliverance.

WEEK TWENTY-SEVEN

Read chapter 27: "His Obedience"
from THE POWER OF A PRAYING WIFE.

1. Do you feel your husband has as deep and committed a relationship with God as you do? Or is it deeper and more committed than yours? Of the two of you, who do you feel needs the most spiritual growth in order to catch up with the other? Write a prayer asking God to help you grow together in the Lord.

2. Do you consider your husband a man of prayer? How much does he pray? Would you like to see him pray more? Write a prayer about that.

3. Do you feel that your husband has a heart to obey God
    and live His way? Explain.

4. Do you ever see your husband doing things that are op-
    posed to the way God has asked us to live? Do you speak
    to him about those things? If so, how does he respond?
    How can you pray for him about this?

5.   Do you believe that praying for your husband first before saying anything, or just praying and not saying anything at all, could have a positive effect on his ability to change? How so? Do you do that?

6.   One of the best ways to learn how God wants us to live is to read His Word. Does your husband read the Bible regularly? Does he get good Bible teaching? Write a prayer below asking God to open your husband's heart to an ever-increasing knowledge of the truth of His Word.

7. Read Matthew 7:24-27 in your Bible and underline it.
    In light of this Scripture, how important is it to you and
    your family that your husband obeys God?

8. Read Proverbs 28:9 in your Bible and underline it.
    What happens when we don't walk in obedience? Does
    your husband experience frustration over unanswered
    prayer? Explain.

9. Read Proverbs 29:18 in your Bible and underline it.
   When we don't have revelation, we get careless. Bad things happen to people because they have no revelation and as a result throw caution to the wind. When we have revelation, we see the wisdom of walking in a manner totally dependent upon God and of living God's way every moment. Write a prayer below asking God to give your husband that kind of revelation and a desire to obey Him.

10. Pray the prayer out loud on page 186 in THE POWER OF A PRAYING WIFE. Include specifics as related to your husband's obedience.

WEEK TWENTY-EIGHT

Read chapter 28: "His Self-Image"
from THE POWER OF A PRAYING WIFE.

1. Do you feel that your husband is living up to his potential? Why or why not?

2. Is your husband's perception of himself that of a successful man, or does he have doubts about himself that creep into his job performance? Explain.

3. Does your husband have feelings of rejection? Did he feel rejected in his past? Does he feel rejected by you? His children? His family members? Does he commonly anticipate being rejected by people? Explain.

4. Does rejection run in your husband's family? Are his family members easily made to feel rejected? Have there been misunderstandings because he or a family member feels rejected? Explain.

5. Do *you* ever have feelings of rejection? Do you ever feel rejected by your husband? Is rejection a part of your past? Explain.

6. Read Ephesians 1:3-6 in your Bible and underline it. Write this Scripture as a prayer for your husband and for yourself.

7. Part of being accepted by other people has to do with accepting who we are in the Lord first. Do you feel your husband accepts himself, or is he hard on himself? Explain. Do you accept yourself or are you hard on yourself?

8. Write a prayer below asking God to help your husband fully receive His love and acceptance and be able to find his identity in the Lord.

9. Read Colossians 3:9,10 in your Bible and underline it. Write this Scripture as a prayer, inserting your husband's name.

10. Pray the prayer out loud on page 192 in THE POWER OF A PRAYING WIFE. Include specifics about your husband's self-esteem.

WEEK TWENTY-NINE

Read chapter 29: "His Faith"
from THE POWER OF A PRAYING WIFE.

1. Do you see your husband as a man who walks in faith to a certain degree in his life? In what ways and to what degree?

2. Sensing our own limitations doesn't mean our faith is weak; feeling that God has limitations indicates weak faith. Do you think your husband believes that God has limitations? How so? Write a prayer asking God to help your husband believe that with God nothing is impossible.

3.   Are you and your husband in agreement about faith in
     God? About belief in the Bible? Are you in unity about
     the church where you worship? Explain. How could you
     pray about these things?

4.   Is your husband's faith in God's love, protection, and
     ability to answer his prayers unwavering, or does he have
     times of serious doubt? Why? How do you feel about his
     level of faith? How would you like to see it change?

5. Read Matthew 17:20 in your Bible and underline it. Write a prayer asking God to help your husband develop the kind of faith that moves mountains so that nothing will be impossible in his life. Pray that for yourself as well.

6. Do you believe that there is nothing in your life or your husband's life that can't be positively affected by having a stronger relationship with God and faith in His Word? Why or why not? What things in particular do you feel would be greatly affected by your husband having a stronger faith in God?

7. Read Ephesians 6:14-16 in your Bible and underline it. Why is the shield of faith important?

8. Read James 1:6-8 in your Bible and underline it. What kind of life are we setting ourselves up for if we are controlled by doubt?

9. Read Romans 10:17 in your Bible and underline it. If faith comes by hearing the Word of God, what is another way you could pray for your husband to increase in faith?

10. Pray the prayer out loud on page 197 in THE POWER OF A PRAYING WIFE. Include specifics about your husband's faith.

Week Thirty

Read chapter 30: "His Future"
from The Power of a Praying Wife.

1. Does your husband feel hopeful about the future? Why or why not?

2. Does your husband have a vision for the future? In other words, even though he may not know specifics about his future, does he have a sense of the direction he's going in and feel good about it? Do you? Explain.

3.   How do *you* feel about your husband's future? Are you
      concerned about it? Do you feel hopeful? Why or why
      not? What could you say to your husband today that
      would help him to feel hopeful about his future? How
      could you pray? Ask God to show you and then do it.

4.   Does your husband have a tendency to get overworked,
      overtired, overwhelmed, burned out, distanced from
      God, or confused about his purpose? Explain why or why
      not.

5. Read Jeremiah 29:11 in your Bible and underline it. Does your husband ever lose sight of his dreams and forget what God says about his future? Explain. If so, how could you help him?

6. Read Romans 8:18 in your Bible and underline it. Do you or your husband forget the glory that is set before you when there is suffering in the present? Give examples. How could you pray about this?

7.   Write down what you think concerns your husband most about his future. Now ask him and see what he says. Did he say the same things you thought he would say? Did he add anything that surprised you?

8.   Write a prayer regarding everything your husband mentioned being concerned about for his future. Tell him you are going to be praying for each one of those concerns.

9. God doesn't want us to know the future. He wants us to know _____ (page 201). If we do that, He can lead us into our future one step at a time. Write a prayer for your husband to know Jesus better.

10. Pray the prayer out loud on pages 201–02 in THE POWER OF A PRAYING WIFE. Include specifics about your husband's future.

Answers to Prayer

What answers to prayer have you seen since you started praying for your husband? Be sure to write them down. It's important to acknowledge what God has done and praise Him for it.

Other Books
by Stormie Omartian

The Power of a Praying® Husband

The Power of a Praying® Husband
The Power of a Praying® Husband Deluxe Edition
The Power of a Praying® Husband Prayer & Study Guide
The Power of a Praying® Husband CD
The Power of a Praying® Husband Prayer Pak

The Power of a Praying® Parent

The Power of a Praying® Parent
The Power of a Praying® Parent Deluxe Edition
The Power of a Praying® Parent Prayer and Study Guide
The Power of a Praying® Parent Prayer Journal
The Power of a Praying® Parent Prayer Cards
The Power of a Praying® Parent CD
The Power of a Praying® Parent Audio Cassettes

The Power of a Praying® Wife

The Power of a Praying® Wife
The Power of a Praying® Wife Deluxe Edition
The Power of a Praying® Wife Prayer and Study Guide
The Power of a Praying® Wife Prayer Journal
The Power of a Praying® Wife Prayer Cards
The Power of a Praying® Wife CD
The Power of a Praying® Wife Audio Cassettes

The Power of a Praying® Woman

The Power of a Praying® Woman
The Power of a Praying® Woman Deluxe Edition
The Power of a Praying® Woman Prayer and Study Guide
The Power of a Praying® Woman Prayer Journal
The Power of a Praying® Woman Prayer Cards
The Power of a Praying® Woman CD

The Power of Praying™ Together

The Power of Praying™ Together
The Power of Praying™ Together Study Guide
The Power of Praying™ Together Prayer Cards
The Power of Praying™ Together CD

Other Items

Greater Health God's Way
Just Enough Light for the Step I'm On
Just Enough Light for the Step I'm On—A Devotional
   Prayer Journey
Just Enough Light for the Step I'm On Prayer Cards
The Power of Christmas Prayer™
The Power of Praying™ Gift Collection
Stormie